OUR FATHER WHICH ART IN HEAVEN, HALLOWED BE THY NAME.

Matthew 6:9 *(KJV)*

These words are the beginning of a prayer Jesus taught us. It's called the Lord's Prayer. "Hallowed" means holy or perfect. God is our perfect heavenly Father who loves us and takes care of us. God listens when we talk to Him. Talking to God is called prayer. What can you say to God when you go to sleep at night?

THY KINGDOM COME, THY WILL BE DONE IN EARTH, AS IT IS IN HEAVEN.

Matthew 6:10 (*KJV*)

God created everything—the mountains and the oceans, animals and people, stars and sun and moon.
What are you especially glad that God created?

GIVE US THIS DAY OUR DAILY BREAD.

Matthew 6:11 *(KJV)*

Because God made us, He knows all that we need. God provides food and water to help us grow up strong and healthy. He gives us families to take care of us.
What would you like to thank God for?

AND FORGIVE US OUR DEBTS...

Matthew 6:12 *(KJV)*

"Debts" mean sins, or things that we do that are wrong. When we do something wrong, we can talk to God. We can tell God we are sorry and ask Him to forgive us. Why does the boy in the picture need forgiveness?

National Day of Prayer

Mrs. Shirley Dobson, Chairman

The annual **National Day of Prayer** comes every year on the first Thursday of May. Americans are encouraged to set aside time for concentrated prayer at work, school, church and home. The National Day of Prayer Task Force, a nonsectarian group with no political affiliation, says it is the right, privilege and responsibility of citizens to pray for America and its leaders, churches, businesses, schools and families.

National Days of Prayer have been observed since colonial days and have become an American tradition. In 1952, the United States Congress unanimously passed a joint resolution that was signed by President Harry S. Truman, establishing the National Day of Prayer by federal law. This law was amended in 1988 and signed by President Ronald Reagan, establishing the first Thursday in May as the official National Day of Prayer. For more than 40 years, American citizens have united for this annual event—rising above denominational differences to lift their thanks, praise and needs before the Almighty Creator.

It is the duty of our nation.

It was Abraham Lincoln who once said: "It is the duty of nations...to acknowledge their dependence upon the overruling power of God...and to recognize the sublime truth, announced in the Holy Scripture and proven by all history that those nations only are blessed whose God is the Lord." Even today, Mr. Lincoln's words echo through the corridors of time and resonate in our hearts. Our country stands at a great crossroad, not unlike the crisis that threatened its stability during the Civil War. Our children are in trouble, our families are disintegrating, our streets are besieged by crime and our people seem to have lost their vision. And as our forefathers asked God for help in that stressful time, we must "seek His face" and ask for His healing mercies in this day of uncertainty. More than ever, let us go to our knees with contrite and humble hearts.

The Adopt-a-Leader program.

Just as our forefathers asked for divine help, it is the duty of Americans today to intercede on behalf of our country's leaders. Consequently, the National Day of Prayer Task Force is especially excited about a new program that has been created called "Adopt-a-Leader." The objective of this program is for individuals and families to select one local, state, or national leader and commit to pray for and communicate with him or her on a regular basis for one year.

To help people get started, the National Day of Prayer Task Force has put together an "Adopt-a-Leader" kit that includes the tools and ideas to make adoption of a leader easy. Included in the kit are a postcard to tell the leader that he or she has been adopted, note cards to encourage the leader each month, a reminder card to help participants pray, and a prayer journal to record prayers and answers. **To order an "Adopt-a-Leader" kit, please contact the National Day of Prayer Task Force at (800) 444-8828.**

God honors our prayers.

God honors the prayers of His people. Therefore, the National Day of Prayer Task Force encourages Americans to pray for and exhort those men and women who carry the heavy burden of guiding our land. The need for folded hands and bended knees in America is greater than ever before and every American—side by side with countless others—can make a world of difference.

...AS WE FORGIVE OUR DEBTORS.

Matthew 6:12 *(KJV)*

God wants us to forgive other people, too. Sometimes it's hard to show love and forgive,
but we can pray and ask God to help us.
When is a time you can forgive?

AND LEAD US NOT INTO TEMPTATION...

Matthew 6:13 *(KJV)*

Temptation is when we want to do things that we know are wrong. God will help us obey Him and stay away from wrong things. We can pray and ask God to help us do what is right.
What is the girl in the picture tempted to do?

GOD HAS SURELY LISTENED AND HEARD MY VOICE IN PRAYER.

Psalm 66:19 (*NIV*)

God is never too busy to listen to our prayers.
You can talk to Him silently or out loud. You can write or draw your prayers.
What do you want to talk to God about?

...BUT DELIVER US FROM EVIL.

Matthew 6:13 (*KJV*)

God loves us and wants to help us. He is always with us.
We can pray to Him whenever we are afraid, sad or worried.
When have you been afraid?

AND THE GLORY, FOREVER. Amen.

Matthew 6:13 (*KJV*)

We can say "amen" at the end of our prayers. Amen means "Yes! It's true!" It's true that we are all in God's kingdom or family. You can pray and thank God for being your Father in heaven and for always listening to you.

IS ANYONE OF YOU IN TROUBLE? HE SHOULD PRAY.

James 5:13 (*NIV*)

We can talk to God any time and any place.
We can pray to Him when we are in trouble or danger. He will take care of us.
Why is this family in trouble?

IS ANYONE HAPPY? LET HIM SING SONGS OF PRAISE.

James 5:13 (*NIV*)

Praising God is telling Him that we love Him and how happy we are about the
good things He's done for us. We can praise God with our prayers, with singing and making music.
What can you praise God for?

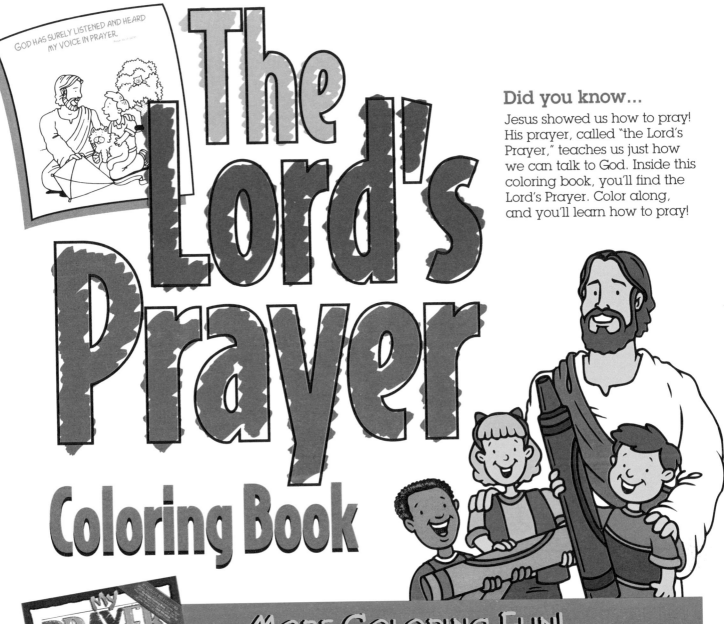

The Lord's Prayer Coloring Book

GOD HAS SURELY LISTENED AND HEARD MY VOICE IN PRAYER.

Did you know...

Jesus showed us how to pray! His prayer, called "the Lord's Prayer," teaches us just how we can talk to God. Inside this coloring book, you'll find the Lord's Prayer. Color along, and you'll learn how to pray!

MORE COLORING FUN!

My Prayer Coloring Book teaches kids that they can talk to God any time they want to! Whether it's day or night, whether they're happy or sad, God will listen to their prayers. Another great coloring book from Shirley Dobson.

There is no greater contribution parents can make to their children than to teach them the power of prayer. Their faith will be an anchor, as it was for me, through all the storms and trials of growing up. This responsibility exceeds every other objective during the parenting years.

—Shirley Dobson

SPCN 2-5116-0898-7

These and other great prayer resources are available at your local Christian bookstore.

Gospel Light

9 782511 608982

900

V0125